Tears of Fire

Tears of Fire

EVAN MYCHAL SMITH

authorHOUSE®

AuthorHouse™
1663 Liberty Drive
Bloomington, IN 47403
www.authorhouse.com
Phone: 1-800-839-8640

First published by AuthorHouse   06/01/2011

ISBN: 978-1-4634-1805-2 (sc)
ISBN: 978-1-4634-1804-5 (ebk)

Library of Congress Control Number: 2011909196

Printed in the United States of America

2013

beware the ides of march
capsizing a ship sailed, the lasting ark
lo and behold the pale horse and grim reaper
the archetypal king of kings, the blonde and thin
Jesus

the rhetoric is evident of final days
as if we've approached and encroached on final
graves
Mayan words were twisted, turned
ancient scriptures ripped and burned

life goes on through hell and fire
without song from bells or choir
Satan's army flees and runs
God is us, the people won

A Mermaid's Kiss

as long as you're underwater, i'll hold my breath
i'd sacrifice my lungs for a mermaid's kiss
bubbles, forming around my mouth like thought
clouds
sending love letters to the surface
i'll be here, wading and waiting with closed eyes
wishing each passing current was your lips against
mine
and again i'd open my eyes to a deep, dark blue
still remembering the way you move, hips for my
hands
moving in between them like waving water
and your hair like feathers on the wings of a fallen
angel
sometimes i want to return to where i came from
up above in the light, sitting on the dock staring
down at your world
but it's a different feeling of freedom, swimming
knowing that one day soon i'll see your face
peeking out from a coral reef, and you'll see me
and smile
i've grown gills made of faith that breathe only of
you
and i breathe deeply, swimming after you

A Slow Ride Into Sleep

With the lights off
And the door closed
All the hormones
Start to change shape

Like the room does
In the shadows
Commence battle
Underneath the skin

The heat rises
So intensely
So immensely
That you're starting to melt

Leaving a puddle
On the mattress
Like an actress
Improvising her lines

You surprise me
With conviction
On your mission
To implode my mind

With your attachment
To my waistline
Like a bass line
Getting into a groove

Evan Mychal Smith

While we're dancing
You make faces
These embraces
Are finally taking a toll

You let me pass through
While you whimper
Like you're injured
Calling me by name

And at your lungs top
A crying shriek
A sigh of relief
A slow ride into sleep

A Nice Guy Like Me

i could never get away with much
a nice guy like me can't afford
to lose what i've built and saved
after all these years

it's a different light i'm under
blinding and close, inquisitive
shining 'i don't think so's
and 'maybe down the line's

where is my reward for walking
on the side of right?
just another tale told, a fable
for the feeble-minded

i tried my hand on the flip side
as cocky as they come
selfish and proud, shrewd
finding similar result

even dressed as a wolf
a sheep is a sheep
and the smart ones can always
smell the difference

A Strange Beauty

how can heaven be a perfect place
when if i died today
i would miss her voice
and her smile
beneath my heavy wings?

do angels cry?

if so, then
sadness must be
perfect as well
jealousy and anger too

it's strange, beauty

as strange as
my weather-beaten heart.
as holding out a dozen roses
with bloody palms,
as saying i love you
to a silent response

An Alternative To You

i'm locked in this lifehouse
in the lowest, darkest corner
of the bottom floor
just thinking about you
and me

i hope you decide
to release me from this place
where I don't belong

let me free out into the world
where the sun is burning bright
so it can shinedown
and light our fire

i would give almost anything
to lock hands with you
and stare into this vertical horizon
while the sounds of crashing waves
echo inside us

underneath a blazing star
you sparkle and shimmer
until the day runs out of fuel

it doesn't have
to be so complicated
see i've got this simple plan
where things don't have to be

Evan Mychal Smith

perfect

but you don't seem to see
the same vision i see
through my wishful eyes

so here i am in this room

three doors down from
where we met

away from the sun and
here
without you

behind these eyes

a transparent gaze
reflection torrential, floating in flood
veiled by an arid shell

and those who seek will find
with little resistance
the weather behind the window

the levees hold strong
under the window sill
here comes the rain

between

Do I ask her if she wants to?
I have no idea what to do
Won't she just know?
She'll probably wait for me to start
I'm worrying too much
I just hope she doesn't think
It'll change what's between us

I know she feels what I'm feeling
She sits there, looking away
I jab her arm, she smiles
And I know
She jabs me in the ribs
Flinching immediately, retreating
Expecting retaliation
Expecting escalation
So I deliver

I pinched her thigh
She kicked me
I grabbed her behind the knees
Pulled them past my waist
She pushed against my chest
Her feet were behind me
They met in the middle
She stretched my shirt
Against the back of my neck
I fell on her
Between her

Screaming and grunting
Yelling and sweating
Pushing and pulling
Rising and falling
Until unable
Shoulders pinning her against the door
Heels digging in to the back of my legs
Exasperating
Turning to let her go

She fell and I pounced on her
My arms extended at her sides

She grabbed my biceps and squeezed
Bending her fingers in
I lowered myself
Lips first, landing on hers
A short exhale
sigh
"Am I still who I was to you?"
You will always be, I said
She smiled

Evan Mychal Smith

Black Is The Worst Color

When a child cries at night
In his room, alone in the dark
He is afraid. The shadows of
his toys and closet doors
come alive and crawl toward
his bed. His heart falls to his
ankles and his lungs capsize
like a ship in a perfect storm.
He longs for the light
in the darkness.
Because black is the worst color.

The smell of death burns.
Not in the same way that a flame
burns a tree branch, but more like
the way that Holy water burns
the soul of a sinner. People
don't even shake hands anymore
to avoid the cold dead hand of
the reaper.
First it was rats. Then it came
for us all. Everyone had a deep
fear of the plague.
Because black is the worst color.

We didn't grow on trees,
we hung from them. Sweet cinnamon
skin dangled from twisted ropes in this
land that was new to us. In a way, we

grew like the trees we became
ornaments on. We were watered with
fire hoses. Even our roses grew from
concrete. And as we grow in unison
on this farm, the gardeners still slash
and burn, unbeknownst to them that
we will grow back faster and stronger.
God gives us perseverance to flourish
under these harsh conditions. Just
to be fair.
Because Black is the worst color.

Evan Mychal Smith

Bloodmarks of the Vampire

We drew the drapes on our secret meeting
Covering every inch of light coming in through the
bedroom window
Then, swallowed in darkness
I had the courage to become one of them
Bloodthirsty fiends, hiding from the light
Confiding only in the unseen
She looked at me with a menacing stare
And before I knew it, the ceremony had begun

The bed's springs struck me in the back
My breath shallow underneath her body
Coupled of course with the fear of crossing over
The transformation from good to evil
A demonic rite of passage

She leaned in
Dripping saliva from lustful lips
I relinquished my head to gravity
I wonder if this is how Dracula started.

Buried

is a diamond still a diamond if it lays under layers
of sediment?
if it's been undiscovered? unappreciated?
the answer is quite clear

what if that diamond could think?
how would it feel?
much like the average rock stepped over by
passersby?

what if that diamond could speak?
would it scream to be saved?
would it strive for attention and celebration of its
features?

i think it would smile sweetly
resting between the rest of the rocks
confident, conscious of its worth

Can

-hey, are you lost?
not anymore, sir . . . but i am afraid
-afraid of what?
them . . . they give us can, sir
-can? what can?
this can, sir
-where did you get that?
they gave it to me
-who?
they gave me can, sir . . . look
-*reads can* . . . the company? they sold it to you?
they just gave me can, sir. i didn't ask for it
-what's wrong with that? it was free
i don't want can, sir
-whatever, where are your parents
they died
-that's terrible, what happened to them?
they also had can, sir.
-get rid of that thing then! That's creepy
can't sir.

Cards

Damn.
Six of clubs.
Three of clubs.
Maybe I could
Bluff my way to victory.
No sixes, threes or clubs
Are showing.
I lose another hand.
I would rather fight it out
Then fold
And hope that my next hand
Is worth going the distance.

Maybe that's the problem.

Here comes a new set.
Pocket deuces.
Not bad.
But there's three spades showing.
I raise the bet in confidence.
It's immediately matched.
I call,
Show my cards
And lose once again
To a family of spades.
The husband and wife
The son
And two children.

Cold As Fall

It was cold
It was fall
Atop a hill I sat alone
Peering down at tiny drones
Scurrying
Lost in worry
Dispersed by the wind

Flags dance
Blades of grass all bow to an invisible God
It was cold
I was cold
Wisps of air sought refuge in my nose
And were largely rejected
Swelling up my lungs rather quickly
Only to be violently evicted
In a tense expulsion

Common Love

bari luis
es hora de despertar
per resistere al dolore di fame
un sacrificio digno
la purezza sostituisce il peccato
demostrar bocas vacías al sol
nous sommes chacun des un famille
coma solamente de amor
fino al tramonto
bari yereko

Daddy's Little Girl

It's natural for me to spoil you
With words I oil you, slippery, toy you
Play with nerves like, 'boy this is a nice game'
Hit the heart, precise aim, with a dart
My ice frame, more like glass, shatters
You incinerate loose fabric, frayed at the ends
I play and pretend, becoming a ball of flames
Burning, it's all the same to you ain't it?
But I won't change it, you say when I change me
That it's not the same me, letting you feel pain, me
Shame me, the prisoner in his own jail
Burning when I own hell, yeah, the devil's boss
Authorized to give raises and throw shells
Duck when the metal's tossed, I spit spiral impact
No more backpedaling to you with grammar and
syntax
So when you lean in for a kiss, I'll make your chin
crack

Come to daddy little girl, rashes and all
Always reaching for the Johnson and Johnson
When it happens to call, you smile
But I'm not laughing at all, you change colors
Like leaves when they snap in the fall
I hear you were on your back in the mall
It's your sport so you practice at all
Times, don't lose your touch, cry
When I play too rough, maybe I said too much

Maybe I said not enough, playing King Midas it
sucks
All of my gold starts to rust, you were never real
You're a bust, I guess abstract art is just such
That can't be explained or summed up
My momma said don't be bitter, you'll lose out
Look what kind of girl some good makes
How can you stand with screws out? Yeah,
Puppy dog eyes, make sure you make that good
face
I'll make sure you stand strong, I'll screw you 'til
the wood breaks

How could I ever think to date or marry you
When you bite my arms when I carry you? How do
you
Feel when I bite back, a man's got to fight back
I'll give it hard when I strike back, it's not gonna be
a light tap
When I bruise you, you boo-hoo, say I'm abusive
But you like that, despite that, and then you're on
the right track
I'll rope you to the right track, and just before the
train come
Ask you about the things you've done for me and
let you name one
But never will a name come, tears of salty rain
drop
You scream to get saved and let the pain stop, it
works
Every single time, I loosen the rope up, you pull
The dagger out from under your blouse, its cat and
mouse

And my throat's cut, choking, I sew myself
Double knotting the ends, just to reopen the wound
in my neck
I scream not again, veins leak, blood in my eyes
Here comes the plot again, Daddy needs one more
try
To make you rot from within

I birthed you ungrateful seed of evil, you bleed
diesel
Highly flammable, yes, my only chance is to
damage
Your chest, ram it with the end of my pen, inking
your
Death once again, thinking it's best when I sin
Murder and pain are my friends, those eyes won't
work
With me dear daughter, while you grin ear to ear
daughter
I'll soon make it clear my dear you'll fear slaughter
The cold is where I now breathe at, it's over when
I react
A razor blade and ski mask, under the tongue, you
see that?
As natural as a thousand herbs and pounds of
curd
My script will slit you, I'll kill you with my nouns
and verbs
You're the proper one, and here come the action
words
And don't forget the bad verbs and adverbs, like
maliciously
Delicious, not magically, more like dastardly

See, the rat bastard me now cares less in comparison
To you currently, and me past, save the face too late
To save face, look around you, the same place
The same mate and that train's got the same plates
This time the rope has changed shape, it's a chain
That I've melted to the track, lie down and relax
You'll soon know where you're at

Bye, bye, baby.

Days

Some days I'll trade an olive branch for a
grapevine
Stretch out on a bed of leaves and be cooled by
waving wrists

Dirty, Dirty

get soiled
life ain't
always clean
roll around
and have fun
feels good don't it?
yeah, get it all in there

let me help
I'll just shovel it all
on there
rub it in
but don't tell
and take a shower
before you go back home

Downhill

chaotic, hurling toward an end
returning to the earth whence it came
this juggernaut is unrelenting
a downhill race
where the winners lay at the bottom
the losers finish where they fall
an avalanche of flesh and skin, intertwining minds
trip and catch legs in its grasp like a rubber web
and suddenly the runners seem more deadly than
the race itself
trampling the weak, the tired, the clumsy, and the
lost
slipping under the moving rocks
triggering the mines hidden under the shade of the
sun
to conveniently claim unsuspecting victims
kicking ribs and limp corpses aside
those who survive the longest
eventually realize
that the race never ends
sunken and drained
dropping to a knee, dry heaving
becoming the terrain

Drown

It was the devastation of a world
One of great potential

They came in with guns blazing
And my resources weren't enough
To hold off the onslaught

I have failed,
A failure in sacrifice
Because resistance is futile
Is infinitesimal

Soon enough I will drown
In my own blood, in my own words
In my own hope

Fuzzy

Everything's fuzzy now
I feel weak
My eyes
They're heavy and I cannot
Hold on any longer
I strain harder and harder and try
To lift them up
But no matter how hard I try
I just can't and . . .

Everything's fuzzy now
And soon it clears slowly
I hear her talking and I listen
Until I can't anymore
The words, they tickle
And hover around my
Ears but they don't
Sink in
And before I can once
Again focus my mind . . .

Everything's fuzzy now
I wonder whether I will
Ever regain control
After the first, second, and
Third time, I lose hope
I can try to fight and
Hold on, but I know its
No use

So here it comes again,
The weakness, my clouded
Head
And everything's fuzzy now.

Evan Mychal Smith

Goodbye In Disbelief

I'm going
I wanna go
Come with me
You sure?
Yeah. Why not?
(Smile in disbelief)

I'm here
Here I am
Door opens
She is breathtaking
Door closes
(Stare in disbelief)

Car stereo
Quiet small talk
Focus on her eyes
Be confident
We're there
(Exit in disbelief)

Inside is packed
Look who it is
This is Evan
Nice to meet you
Buying drinks
(Party in disbelief)

Bottoms up!

Here take this
It's free, hurry up
She's pretty isn't she?
More than she knows
(Speak in disbelief)

Hold her
Touch her shoulders
She lights up
Let's go
I don't dance
(Laugh in disbelief)

Is this real?
Am I just lucky?
She's with me
Wanting me here
Enjoying my company
(Wonder in disbelief)

More than beautiful
She's impressive
I want more
Maybe next week
Meet again
(Hope in disbelief)

Time races
I gotta go
Let's do this again
Just call me
Kiss her cheek
(Goodbye in disbelief)

Graduation

Sincerely, not yours
I never loved you
I just wanted to tell you that
It's been a long time
I've been waiting
I'm ready now

happy birthday

celebrating in reds and blues
flashing, party lights on top of a car
across the street I watch from the asphalt
as the officer walks up and knocks

he rolls down the window, handing over
the paperwork, nervous and reluctant
seventeen minutes pass but he's free to go

i wish i were as free

denim scraping against the parking lot
leaning against a brick

soon I'll be asleep
alone again
waking to this
always returning to this

happier

once upon a time, I met a man who told tales
tall, long-winded fables about animals
numbers, weather and such
he sat low on the sidewalk, leaning on
the pole of a yellow street sign that read "yield"
everybody ignored him for the most part as
he called out loudly, buggy-eyed
making hand gestures and shouting his stories

sometimes a man or woman would stop
and listen to the man speak, but it was children
who loved his stories. they would walk back
from school with their backpacks heavy
set them down on the sidewalk, and sit
against the maroon brick wall of the corner
grocery store. they listened in amazement
every ear was fixed on his voice

and one day I saw the children
lined up, sitting against the brick wall
waiting for the man to come and I took
a seat and scooted backward up against
the street sign and told them a story

I began the shortest story I knew, "there was
a boy who couldn't be happier, spoiled with all the
things in the world. he had a big loving family, a
house full

of toys and a big sister who he spent his summers with
running around, being mischievous

he couldn't be happier he thought, waking up early
on his ninth birthday. there was no one there
to greet him, only a note on the side of his pillow
explaining that his mother was in the hospital
giving birth to a baby boy. he couldn't be happier he
thought, on the evening of the twenty-fifth of August
when he received a phone call that his mother was in
the hospital, giving birth to another baby boy

and as he grew older, the toys became theirs,
his happiness became theirs, his love
became theirs. he now shared with his sister
the feeling of looking
at a younger piece of yourself with pride
and he couldn't be happier

Hate Me

if you're gonna hate me
don't do it half-assed
hate me and hate hard
then hate me harder
until your subconscious
is dominated by vendetta

do it right if you're gonna do it
wish me all of the world's ills
sickness, poverty, and injury
so that I might suffer and fall
and crumble before your eyes

all of what I hold dear
take it all from me piece by piece
until I am bare and lifeless
begging for your mercy

come after me with great rage
and boiling blood, hate
let it consume you
let nothing stand in your way

but while I lay vulnerable
unsuspecting,
underneath your killing blow
how will you destroy
your own creation?

heat~seeking

the sun outstretches a hand
to which I turn my back
inundated with black blood
burning, stinging and spreading
through my bloodstream

a flowing pain, a constant pain
a familiar pain acts to consume me whole
as time passes, it rises—clogging
my senses and rewiring my nerves
locking my lips and lowering my brow

I am heat-seeking regret,
sorrow and vengeance, all of whom
answer the call and visit at once
to draw the blinds

Heaven to Hell

i wanna keep it one-hundred
i play the game
you know the game i'm talking about
people say, 'i dont play games'
i'm grown, i'm above all that
i'm a real bitch, i'm a real dude
i'm cool with the way i am
there's nothin you can tell me
i wake up every morning
with my balls in my hand
giving not a shit what you think
well, congrats

i know what it feels like
to be on the receiving end
to be looked over, passed on
shit, i ain't mad, why would i be?
i've learned that either you're shit
or you're THE shit
and it's easy to find out
which way someone sees you

if i can insult you
disrespect you
lie to you
ditch you
leave you out to dry
abuse you
make you upset

ignore you
torture you
cut you deep
and still have you there
i know where i stand

it's that simple

i've bent over backwards
lied to myself
ran when i couldn't walk
cried in front of my boys
spent money i didn't have
went against my friends
went against my parents
went against my personal views
hurt other people
masked my own feelings
covered for you
told excuses for you
and held you down
no matter how you treated me
right or wrong
i had your back

so crucify me
nail my hands
speak ill will of me
wish death or worse
i've seen bigger
i've seen badder
i've seen pain
i've seen impossible

Evan Mychal Smith

i've seen relentless
your bullets are plastic
your poison is water

when you've always leaned
on your own two legs as crutches
when you've always breathed
into your own lungs as CPR
when you've always stood
in front of the mirror for consolation
there's isn't a demon wicked enough
to lower Heaven to Hell

my shit is flower soil
my footsteps are world wonders
my signature is worth millions
my laugh cures disease
my touch saves lives
and if you disagree
you could either move
or get ran
the fuck
over
period.

hunger

she was the most beautiful girl in the world
she birthed the monster I've become
her head dripped of cascading black diamonds
eyes of the Devil's—but I knew not then
when my soul relinquished, I gutted myself
I, now a shell, was starving, hollow
with nothing to swallow or regurgitate
I ached for weeks, licking my own skin
it was then that I lost control

I ran after one
she didn't resist much I had had her pinned
she was quiet for most of it
wincing in a helpless voice
I sank my teeth into her, spitefully
soon realizing it wasn't enough

she was the most beautiful girl in the world
a reflection of my addiction, sweet
her lips ruined my life in their absence
she was the first and the only
her memory lies in the remains of my tattered soul
along with the seal of restraint

my tongue became a poisoned blade
swung with reckless abandon
the more I taste the more I want
wounding and paralyzing victims
sinking a virus deep into their veins

Evan Mychal Smith

I'm a remorseless creature
with unraveling fabric of mind
fraying, tearing and loosening
locking me away in this corpse
this hunger is unrelenting
I'm continuously starving for the kill
she is the most beautiful girl in the world
I am but a malfunctioning machine
eating through the pain

hydroplane

rubber-less tires
in the pouring rain, soaking
the streets, saturated

every crevice full
it lifts and pushes up
to drip and pool

the faster i drive
the storm worsens
precipitating in response

gripping the wheel firmly
i brake and hydroplane
shifting into reverse

Evan Mychal Smith

i wanna be

i wanna be what you talk about
when you get home, smiling haughtily
"guess who's number I just got?"
the envy of your friends

i wanna be the birthday card
that you read over and over
crying more and more each time

i wanna be the shirt you buy
and wear five times that week

i wanna be the only song you know
on piano, every note—same finger

i wanna be the pair of jeans
that you didn't think could still fit

i wanna be the mirror you look into
that leaves your outer out of it

i wanna be the middle school drawing
up on the refrigerator, held by the magnet
that you got on your favorite vacation

i wanna be the sex you had
that made you feel like a virgin again

i wanna be what you think about
when you get the chills and flushed skin

i wanna be the guy that makes your boyfriend
act right, because he knows he's one strike away

i want my name to be an action word
not just a person, place, or thing

i want to collect the Rockies of Colorado
the pouring rain of the tropical rainforest
the Eiffel tower, Buckingham Palace
the pyramids of Giza, the Great Wall of China
The Statue of Liberty, Niagara Falls
Aurora Borealis and a lunar eclipse
and combine them to fit around your finger, one
day

i wanna go to pick a flower tomorrow
and realize that there are no more
because i drew our names across the Earth
with every petal that exists
and someday i'll take you to the Heavens
so you can see what i've done

i want to create an instrument
that plays the sound of your voice
master it and perform in front of a sold-out crowd
so the world could also hear what i hear

i wanna be what i've always been
so i guess i wanna be alone

i Miss You

tapping a screen, waiting.
stretching a smile, thinking.
tapping a screen, smiling.
thinking, waiting, smiling.
tapping a screen, waiting.
waiting. waiting. thinking.

Imperfect Stranger

Funny how you seem so familiar
Almost like I knew you in a past life
You were sweet then, so convincing
Even after all the lies I've heard
You were supposed to be different
You're not . . .
You're just like her
Such an embarrassing comparison
One farmer to another, it seems
And I am the harvested

in memory

slowly, dying to live
clutching my chest
feeling a faint tempo
unshaken, disillusioned
for death is life

we are all dying, to live
since life is a draining death
consuming us when it is empty
and life is no more—we are no more
scattered remains in memory

just~this

it's poetic, just-this
a beautiful thing that i desire

just-this; of the peace,
liberty and freedom, i value
it with the utmost
passion

just-this is served
arbitrarily it appears
at its own speed
or not at all

in just-this i spend my thoughts
generously, and my anger
frustration and doubt

just-this, and most people
take advantage of it, ruin it
destroying it's worth

but not me

i've waited too long
and fought too hard
to give up, i'm going to
get just-this in due time

like death

you know when you feel that
nagging pain and you go, hmm . . .
i should do something about this
and you do . . . suddenly you feel
so much better about everything
and you smile and you laugh
so much more than you used to
and people notice . . . and they go
"you seem so happy now"
and you go "yeah i am!"
you watch your favorite shows
you wear your favorite clothes
you eat your favorite foods
then the night falls on top of you
and everything slows down
and you get ready for bed
and you lay down and you
pull the covers up to your shoulders
and you feel like death

Like to love

I remember what it was like to love
The best thing in life I'd put it right above
Forget that, a first-class flight above!
Bright, in a dark night we'd spark like a lightning bug
Sure I had my gripes with love but nothing's like to love
This . . . exciting love and never hiding love
Had me nursery rhyme writing love, even when she left me a little red
Riding love . . . Oh what it was like to love, so fast
A lightning strike to love, oh so much I liked to love
That if there was an everlasting hike to love
I would run, or ride my bike to love all day and all night to love
At times it felt like a disease that I was dying of
And I cried in love, "You false advertising, lying love!
So young, why am I trying love?" I reached for the sky to love
So high that nothing could fly above my eyes in love
I swear there must be some Russian spies in love or mob ties in love
Because while in love I was hit with bullets the size of love
The fragility is that you may not realize in love had me

With not enough money to get by for love, so I was
on the grind for love
Working at a desk from 10-5 for love, watching the
dining hall meal cards slide for love
Checking the hot box for more fries . . . all just to
get money to be by her side . . . my love
Some of my girl friends asked me "Why, my love? I
mean it's nice my love
But what won't you sacrifice, my love?" I'd rather
fall victim to the knife of love
If I lose, I know I did all I could to fight for love
I had to look good, keep it tight for love
On pizza, I wouldn't even snack a slice for love
On that scale I was getting all light for love
Thought I was earning all my stripes for love
But then came that fateful night, my love
Said that it wasn't out of spite, but that for me she
felt like, not love
And that like turned to not quite like
From love, I fell and landed on the spikes of love
She never again crossed my sight and that's been
my entire life in love
No longer am interested in the hype of love
Or quest to reach the great heights of love
Since then, I've never felt right to love
In fact, I wouldn't even really like to love

Location Location Location

consolation lies here in this glass
a reflection projected clearly
mimicking my every move
staring with the same look
dejected and detached

comfort lies here on the ground
an outline darkened in
growing and shrinking
never straying from my footsteps

strength lies here in my chest
encasing a vile poison
quarantined for good it seems
in order to save the body
from confusion and searing pain

escape lies here in my mind
the creator of dreams and fantasy
a vacation home for the rich
where time has no measure
and truth holds no merit

reality lies here
at the intersection of opinion and fact

Evan Mychal Smith

between love and reason
colliding with selfishness and sacrifice
nestled in the corner of truth and lies
somewhere in the middle
of a question and its answer

Mama

the product of a broken mold, indeed
an experiment gone awry
where there would normally
be fear, there is confidence
and faith takes the place of doubt

a mutation perhaps, a glitch
in the programming, maybe
for what else could explain
such an undying determination
to succeed beyond limit, destroying
the psychological constraints that plague
and brainwash this world of tender minds?

what shall be done about this warrior
who fights on the front lines in the army
of the good? human, yet invincible
it is said that the strong survive
and that a mother's love is powerful
beyond compare

from birth I have been marked by the
warm graces of God, trusting that I
will learn from and honor the legacy
set before me, and gratefully
and gracefully carry on

man made

angles for angels and fraud for God
crooked are books and given is took
look at us, look
blindfolded and mind-molded
invented incentives, presented potential
labor is favors and debt is dead
man made maze and man made slaves
man made pain and man made paid
man made shades of gray
disobedience—sick ol' deviants
unlock and watch
the end of man's slaughter
the land of Pandora

lucky

this bed is colder than it's ever been
and i can't sleep

a gentle yet icy wind blows—it seems,
rolls over my skin and causes me to
shiver and tighten up

curling my knees to my chest
sliding my face down a soft
bitter pillow, it just becomes
too much to bear

i get up and turn on my heater
and place it directly beside
my bed

i put my hands to the front of it
to make sure that it's turned on
and i pull my blanket over my trembling
shoulders, rolling over to a side

after a few minutes
i feel as cold as i was when i first
climbed in

i soon realized that the heater
will not work, because i am the type
of cold that chills from the inside

Evan Mychal Smith

dark clouds start to form
behind my eyelids and to avoid
snowfall, i shut them tight

and stay still hoping to drift off
because maybe if i'm lucky,
i'll be warm in my dreams

Mine

It is mine what I own
It is mine, mine alone
In my mind, it is sewn
It's online, on the phone

It is mine what I own
It is mine, mine alone
In my mind, it has grown
I'm still finding my tone

It is mine what I own
It is mine, mine alone
In my mind, I have known
I'm behind such a stone

I'm alive, not a drone
I've been taught, follow cones
Eat my words, swallow bones
But it's mine, mine alone

Miss

miss
to miss is to be without
for temporary
a fracture in time
miss
excuse me
but I want to change everything you know
when I tell you how much I
miss
you
are the answer to the question that traps me
here
so I fear, my darling that I
miss
you too much
more than I thought
more than I ought to
miss
my flight to the stars is in your eyes
thinking among your thought clouds
living in between your lips and mine
when my eyes open I'm here and I
miss
feeling your heartbeat in my own chest
counting beats
and I know you're here when I miss
one

my best friend

rolling stops and swaying car slightly
missing turns and forgetting direction
we stop, on the highway to pee
laughing and rejoicing, my best friend
we should write I said, he agreed
but such intense emotion comes
from sadness and despair, no I said
this I feel is more powerful
a smile with everlasting lips
that curl to the sky
a meniscus, and I am full

I lean back and listen
as he speaks, my friend
swimming to the top of liberty
free we are, sovereign
released from binding
moved by God guidance
enjoying creation with fervor

grab another can of altering
as we begin to fly,
spinning and soaring
never returning to land.

Not Responding

it is 3:30am
I will work at 9am
I will jog at 7:30am
I wake up at 7am
or lie awake until-

like a computer that cannot shut down
without closing the programs running
these eyes like automatic doors
pulling open when a thought comes close
closing only in periods of peace
few and far between

a pillow collapses in the middle
so I fold it once and slide it under my neck
it is no use, I remove the pillow
from underneath my neck and clutch it
to my stomach, watching it rise and fall

Only To Reminisce

It's still there
Sitting in my drawer
I rarely go inside it
Only to reminisce

I've got pictures of me when I was younger
Pictures of my friends back in middle school
Old concert tickets and things I got on vacation
Well, that's where I got it from
I was in Orlando. It was Epcot, I remember
I didn't have much money
But I walked into this gift shop
And saw a clear-blue bracelet
A ring of tiny little bears
So I bought it, it wasn't expensive
But my feelings are never cheap

I went back to the room at the resort there
Looked at the clear plastic bag and wondered
How I would give it to you. I thought
Maybe I would meet you in between classes
Surprise you at your locker with it, I was confident
that it would make you smile
That's all I really wanted. It was way after high
school when I told you
I still had it, sitting in my drawer
You told me that you smiled
From the other side of a computer screen
I believed you, and again I thought

How would I give it to you?
Maybe we would meet up on Christmas break
Sometime before school starts up again and I'd
give it to you
You already knew it was coming, I was hoping it
would still be special
And that your boyfriend wouldn't mind
I'm sure you could explain it

Today I hid my sorrows
I'm not very good at it, but I was doing alright
Until I spoke to you and somehow I knew
That you would do exactly what you did
You gave me a smile much bigger than today
I forgot everything, all of it, in an instant
And at that moment all I could think about was
that
I still had it
Sitting in my drawer

I imagined being across from you at some fancy
place
I'm so much older now, much more confident than
my former self
But staring at you from across that table made me
15 again
You smiled, knowingly, and I got up
Put my hand in my pocket and pulled out your
bracelet
I walked over and stood in front of you asking you
for your hand
And you gently placed it in mine I stretched the
bracelet over your wrist

And held your hand tightly after

I know it might not, and probably won't happen
like that
But what I do know is that it will happen
And that I still have it
And it, along with my feelings for you
Still sits in my drawer
And I rarely go inside it

Only to reminisce

Open Your Eyes

Looking back I clearly see what it is that's killing
me

Blind rage and reckless abandon
Rain like a sun-shower
Massive gunpowder shooting through cannons
Plannin', to find the inner me and reprogram him
With a code that'll pave a new road
A wave of new modes to test out
These pulling nerves got me stressed out
But for art's sake it brings my best out
A twisted heartbreak that wrings my chest out
Cavity, hole
Balanced a force that gravity stole
Imagining a soul battered and swollen
Marks reminding me of my patterns of old

Through the eyes of one I know, I see a vision once
let go

Pixie Dust

you still waiting on Santa Clause aren't you?
staying up all night baking cookies, making sure
you leave a few for him on the table
with a warm glass of milk and a letter
telling him all you want for Christmas
and when you wake up that morning
you'll have gifts all around the tree
with your name on them won't you?

how about the Tooth Fairy?
money under the pillow
and you didn't even see her do it
it's the pixie dust, that's the trick
a little sprinkle and 'poof'
the magic takes over
and you wake up grinning
with a snaggletooth smile

what goes around comes around
and what comes around
goes back around right?
because that boss that fired you
tripped and sprained his knee
that's what he gets
for screwing you over

karma's no pushover
but there's a trick, it's the pixie dust
see things happen to good people

Evan Mychal Smith

and things happen to bad people
all the time, but when things happen to you
'poof'—somebody is responsible
but don't worry, that pixie dust will get 'em

there's that one girl for you
oooh she's so beautiful and sexy
her smile gives you butterflies
in your stomach and you can't even speak
you two been talking for a while now
and you want her so much, you really do
there's just something about her, isn't there?
it's love, real love
that's that pixie dust again
working the magic of ignorance

Pizza's On Me

Last night, I found out that you were real
I fell from the sky, walked down that long hallway
And saw you there
Sitting, waiting
I dropped my bags
Ran up behind you and said
"Excuse me, have you seen my baby?"
You turned, jumped, and squeezed me
You, touched me
Your body was pressed against mine
I felt you
You were real
And all the evils of the world
Disappeared
Life was now perfect
And you let me go
Looked into my eyes
And said "I want pizza baby"
I laughed and pulled you in
Close again, even tighter this time
Bent down slightly and kissed you
Sweetly on your soft, tender lips
You looked up longingly with wet eyes
And I said,
"Pizza's on me"

pounding drums and screaming harmonies

sitting in front of the screen
i am, i've been, i will be
iTunes alone
listening loudly
hearing completely
feeling painfully

my song, my song
this song must be . . .

pounding drums and screaming harmonies
looking me in my face almost
as if they are singing to me, about me

my left eye cries, pouring
i resist a wiping reflex
in the name of nature

i am not okay
something is broken

these pounding drums and screaming harmonies
comfort me
yelling echoes inside, past flesh and through bone

nodding my head in agreement at times
to an invisible party—i'm not crazy

i am not okay
something is broken
i am not okay

?

since love is out of the question
like a sentence beyond the mark
beyond the curved line with the dot
can we be with no brand?

if a rose by another name
smells the same
and the stem remains
with petals intact
then what's wrong with that?

what comes first
the friend or the boy?
if rearranged or discarded
you can still be
open-hearted

open-minded with closed eyes
seeing as though we know
that whatever you name you choose
it will be said without sound

Re: In Carnation

The past of us was to be the last of us
Unceremoniously turned ash to dust
What more could be asked from us?
Tending to broken bones once the ladder crushed

Who ever thought of a latter us?
From former, a luke-warmer, but even badder us
They say the candy's even sweeter when the wrapper's rough
And you know if I have the chance I won't pass it up

My prize, again rise like Lazarus
Chains and gates break, scrape off the casket's rust
Come close and give me some of that passion stuff
The truth is you never really had enough

You told me, so bold, me
Things to console me
To fix the hole, me
Not the whole me
Temporarily only
Yes, I was lonely
All alone, me
Because of you I've grown me
Since the message that you showed me

Evan Mychal Smith

And that message sent
After all hell's lament
Hit deep as hell's descent
Perfect sound as bells unbent

I shall not sit idle, I'm
Built up inside in stifled sighs
I'll just issue my reply

Deep dark red
I picked it myself

Regeneration

i never saw it coming
though it had come before
in a similar fashion
in a similar period of time

i thought i was frozen over
such bitterness had taken hold
back when i turned the knob left
until my chest became ice

why then do i feel this now?
an involuntary thawing
warming my core intensely
flooding to my brain

it begins again, i presume
a regeneration of muscle
vulnerable but willing
to risk it all again

Rewind

you left me when i needed you
you turned away, i wanted you
you bit me, i was feeding you
but now, my dear, im haunting you
your dreams are mine, your soul as well
a piece of mind, a hole to hell
no shelter from the cold, a shell
your skeleton to fold, a spell

to cast, wishing you see my eyes
the emptiness in my demise
the bloodshot nights that i lie still
my memory, a time to kill
window ajar, i climb to sill
swimming, gasp behind the gills

as my eyes roll inside my head
from back to front and back again
i yearn to freeze, contain myself
i thought watching the rain would help
as dark as clouds collected in
knew i should have expected this
everlasting pain to bear
press rewind and take me there

Safe

Hit one right in the gap and take the first base,
yeah.
Feels good doesn't it?
No worries at all.
It's comfortable ain't it?
Safe.
No dirt on your jersey.
Take a lead if you want to.
Who's gonna throw you out?
Nobody's in the infield.
Nobody's in the outfield, either.
You could keep running, sure.
But why? What's the rush?
Ain't nobody chasin' you.
And besides,
You have all the innings in the world
To bring it home and score the winning run.
Take a walk back to the batter's box.
Swing that bat like only you know you can.
Yeah, square those shoulders and hit it hard.
Keep your eye on the ball and pull it.
Watch out for the pitcher.
Some pitchers want you to hit it so bad
That they'll throw you a meatball right over the
plate.
Some pitchers are creative.
Throwin' curveballs right on the corner of the
plate.

Some throw it so fast you'll never even see it coming.
Strike one,
Strike two,
Strike three.
Lucky for you the world will never run out of pitchers.
And you can strike out all you want.
Some pitchers get tired of throwing
So always swing at the first pitch.
Hit it like you mean it.
But don't swing for the fences
Unless you're ready to end the game early
Just enough to get to first base.
Safe.

Scribbles

Floating faces were sorrowful there
Smiles were scarce save for mine—this was no prison
But there I was among them
Tangled in ink, surrounded by paper walls
I wrote scribbles to pass the time

It can be hypnotizing if you let it
I imagined walking with words on blue roads
Between avenues of red
For hours upon hours

Perhaps it was a prison
A voluntary yet inescapable cell
That I had grown accustomed
That I had willingly endured
In which you provided muse

I often scanned the walls to find you
Under the guise of wander
When I did, you would be stuck in your own pages
And I would be stuck in gaze

When you looked up I'd walk over
We would talk and smile
And I would return to my scribbles disconnected

Evan Mychal Smith

I sat then, crossing out
Marking and dotting
Looping and twirling
Until I came up with these
Scribbles of you

See/Saw

The rotting wood creaked beneath them
As they sat facing each other
Under the bright, watchful eye of the moon
His eyes met hers along the length of the board
Separated by the darkness of night
Thick, black, comforting
The ends of her lips curled upwards
To form a smile as
Mud rushed between her toes
/ She pushed off of the ground and rose high in the
air
Where the crisp, brown leaves touched her hair
And gently fell to the ground
His shadow soon rose
And hers descended
The crickets' serenade was gradually
Replaced by the warm chirping of the robins

sexiest man alive

if beauty were quantified by one's ability
to paint linguistic works of art with a twirl of the
wrist
to reproduce life in the palm of one's hand
to collapse reality and construct history
to compose and manipulate all senses—to write
i would be chased by ravenous women
heralded, like a king, immortal
i would be the sexiest man alive

if celebrated in such fashion,
this power i wield in my veins would spill and catch
fibers
drying up to become feelings, objects, and moments
in time
replacing abdominal display with versification
flexed biceps with perfectly performed poetry
fashionable wear with lyrical style
then how could you resist falling for my type?
the veritable dreamboat

clay worlds i mold
in saliva and blood
in precision and love
commanding existence with hands and tongue
speaking tears of joy
a talent unmatched, the writer's gift
architects of the nervous society

pulling strings for the world
behind curtains made of ink and paper

my song unsung sings volumes
let it be known that it is all poetry
an axis tilted on ballpoint
revolving in time and space
every raindrop in a puddle
every break-up
every repressed memory
is at my fingertips

Evan Mychal Smith

She Loves Me Knot

When the first petal fell, we fell together
When the last petal fell, we helped each other up
She curled the stem into a circle
Pushed one end through the middle and
Gently pulled at the ends
She wore the knotted stem over her ear

Solve For Ex

Are you in your room?
If not, make your way back to your room
Close the door, remove your jacket
And whatever else renders you uncomfortable
Set it aside
This moment has no room for distractions

I know you like to busy, scheduled
But for now, right now
Close your eyes and focus
Just on the here and now
There is nothing due tomorrow
Your friends aren't looking for you
There is nothing going on outside
Of the door of your room
Tonight has no room for distractions

Turn off the lights
Except for the dimmest one
That will allow you to read these words clearly
Close the window
Turn off your phone
Lie down and stretch out
And read closely
Your mind has no room for distractions

The room will get warm
You will breathe heavily
Thinking, longing

And your brain will send
Tingling chills
Down your neck
Between your shoulder blades
And out through your arms
And legs
Embrace it
Your body has no room for distraction

You know that I can give you
What you want
Your hands feeling the tension
In my upper arms as I am above you
Pushing against resistant springs
Staring into the middle
Of your eyes
You are all that I want right now
And you know it
And you smile, because
Your feelings have no room for distraction

Think for me
About the last man
That you gave your all to
And compare him to me
His willingness to compromise
His ability to truly give you everything
His appreciation of you, for being you
Taking the good
With the bad
And loving both
And consider me
Can you solve for ex?

I'm sure you can
Your heart has no room for distraction

Open your eyes now
Turn on your phone
Open up the window
Put on your jacket
And swing open the door to your room
Remember your homework
Your job, your friends
Your grades and your future plans
Remember the stress
The drama and the heartache
And remember how five minutes of me
Made it all disappear

Evan Mychal Smith

"Soundtrack to my heart"

from the middle of the stands
i clap with wet hands, wet-
because they are directly
below my chin

i am watching something incredible.

closing my eyes i see through
the dark cascading waterfall
that begins at your scalp and ends
at your back, the subtle passion
in your voice that shakes the ground
beneath my feet—your whisper
that sends nerves shooting through my body
bending, twisting, colliding and
collecting besides my spine—your laugh
a gentle warmness, repeating

the soundtrack to my heart

to which you dance in slow-motion
(the crowd fades out of vision)
its just you and me-
with every beat of my heart you change direction
waving your hips, kicking your legs
and extending your arms
in perfect rhythm

one, one-two
one-two, one-two, one-two, one-two

and it grows faster
and the room begins to shrink
and i begin to sweat
and it gets harder to breathe and
i panic, reaching up to wipe my forehead
when you notice me staring, watching
and you stop

completely dead in your tracks
with a small shiver of the knees
we catch eyes and you look away
down toward the floor, then up toward
the stage lights, and you smile at me
waving me on and i take off running
hopping over auditorium seats,
hitting the open aisle in full stride,
leaping on to the corner of the stage
and you pull me up by my hands,
wrap them around to the back
of your waist and kiss me like it was
the last kiss we would ever have

we interlocked fingers
and i let go of your hands
that were reaching up
to touch my lips
there i was again
in the middle of the crowd
watching as the music stopped
and the applause roared

whistles and pounding feet
and you took a bow as flowers
were tossed around your feet

i clapped until my palms ached
and walked down the rows
turning to the double doors
and i took one last look
at the greatest thing i had ever known
and pushed open the double doors
to the outside of the arena

in your smile i found love
the kind that faith resides in
in your heart i found belonging
confidence and persistence
in your words i found strength
and undying affection

there is no end
to every second we spend
talking about our days
or falling asleep to each other's voices
we just get better
i'll just get better
but i'll always be yours

Stealing Third

I dug my cleats deep into the dirt
waiting for the liberating crack of wood
the silence was deafening
the pitcher wound up and the batter swung
I took off with pistons pumping
grinding with full extension toward third

I was making great speed, gasping
for each breath with eyes closed
prying them open, a fuzzy third base came
into view, a smile splashed across my face
identical to that of the third baseman
with the ball in his glove, waiting

I didn't bother to slide, it was too late to turn back
slowing up, I strode over, surrendering
my shoulder to his glove
jogging dejectedly to an empty dugout

Evan Mychal Smith

Such Bitches

This bitch

I'm coming home
Call me, text me
No answer
I'm leaving now

This bitch

Grab my ass
How do you want it?
You're my best friend
I love you

This bitch

Pick me up, we'll go out
That was so much fun
Let's do it again
Or not

This bitch

I haven't seen you in forever
Come see me
Take me baby
I was just flirting

This bitch

I know you want me
I want you too
My boyfriend doesn't have to know
I never said I liked you

This bitch

I apologize for what I did
I'm truly sorry
Will you forgive me
When I do it again?

Such bitches.

Syracuse

Syracuse I'm too old to change my ways.
Welcome to Syracuse you said, August 23, 2006.
You didn't tell me you were a frigid, insensitive bastard.
Go screw yourself with your lake effect snow.
It's spring for God's sake!
Syracuse have you forgotten that I came here to learn?
Why must you torment me with useless assignment after useless assignment?
I'm too tired to do homework, let me get drunk!
I'll learn much more from the bottom of a bottle than your Geology 105.
I can think of 151 reasons why I fall asleep in your classes.
Why must you patronize me with your demeaning classifications?
Do you think it feels good to be called a freshy, sophomoric, or to be someone's junior?
Syracuse can I get into heaven with an S.U.I.D?
Or do I have to stand outside, call Jesus, and have Him sign me in?
Syracuse I will be tens of thousands of dollars in debt when I stroll off of your hallowed grounds.
I detest waiting for your buses.
When can I walk into the Schine Bookstore and buy what I need with good intentions?
I cheat on every test I can.

Syracuse spare me the false sense of security.

In this economy, what good is a Writing degree?

I will never again go to your football games.

Syracuse I want to major in bullshit artistry!

Is this some sort of four-year game show that makes me the fool at the end of it?

I've never even met Chancellor Clinton, or whatever her name is.

If scholarship is in action then what the hell is mine doing?

Syracuse I don't know what's worse, FOX News or the Daily Orange.

I can't stand the Daily Orange.

Syracuse I don't fit in here.

I pick up girls in your libraries and do obscenely loud homework assignments in your dormitories.

Syracuse why don't you also put laxatives in your lesson plans?

Syracuse one night at approximately 3:26am after I left a masquerade party with just my phone in my pocket and a poorly colored mask in my hand a Department of Public Safety Officer drove past a crowd of drunk partygoers and pulled up next to me and asked me where I had been and said that he got a call that a black male with a mask had been breaking into apartments and stealing electronics but I was wearing shorts and a t shirt where the hell would I have put it?

Syracuse offer me a teaching job as a professor when I graduate.

Syracuse I embrace academic dishonesty.

Syracuse where are the Black fraternity houses?

Syracuse I am Felix Paulino.
I don't want to be your prodigal son, a generous
Carmelo, immortalized Davis.
Syracuse I'm done playing spades.

tear duct tape

restless, laying face down
it doesn't count if one just slips out
pushing the pile over the lid
but when the rest follow, free falling
to catch a cheek and settle in
acceptance is all that's left
so you turn over, seeking solace
in sleep, staring straight up into darkness
fighting, trying to hold it together
with tear duct tape

Evan Mychal Smith

The Dark Art

at the apex of latex
preparing for safe sex
anxiously awaited like late checks
nerves thicker than ape necks
she unsnaps, displays chest, full support
her shape's best, ready to work magic
the dark art, like Snape's test

beneath a thin skirt, I insert, she grins
chills, the needles and pins work
swimming in sin, behind her fins lurk
steaming, winter's invert
refuse relent until skin hurt
the falling wood, timber
while releasing whimper

with spine she ironed sheet
as I split like kick from Tynes feet
i roared through lion's teeth
and caress lioness, incline heat
i grind behind to find deep
until thighs leak, repeat
kiss, a loving stare before eyes sleep

the sandman

the ghost of you lingers around my fat cells
bulging and protruding—it disgusts me
like great waves of wet sand, clumped
the aftermath of stomped castle
pushed together in a mound

i try to rinse you off in sweat
ridding my soul of your cursed grip
but no matter how much of you leaves
more of you comes back
to stick and clump and sit

spilling over into a navel
undulating, crashing into skin
you are a constant reminder
of my position half-way up a meter stick
a slab of slop adds up
in all the unwanted ways

this dried love, like you
was never something i could button
fasten across my waist
or pull over to stretch through

every pat on the belly
packs it on, every poke in jest
i become this swollen sob story
building a castle, only
to have it washed away again

The Show

Ahhhh yes,
welcome.

Welcome all to the fabulous
extravagant battle of the adolescent powerless.
Follow this trip as saliva drips from howling lips
before it's swallowed, licked and gargled
sipped, and spit on the bottom of this marble pit.

These monsters don armor and harbor horror,
showing you the meaning of sorrow like Sweeney
the demon barber, ripping these beasts into
pieces
souls release, leave 'em to Jesus, Father. Let's get it
fleeting
this evening can't wait to see arteries bleeding,
there's no rules
so no cheating, I picked my funeral seating, so
scenic

so I can see 'em go

lay back and relax, everyone see the show

This Morning

This morning
I stopped time.
The clouds sat in the sky
With nowhere to go
The leaves were motionless
Stiff and bent in their previous positions
I gazed out the window
To see the people frozen in their strides
And the cars halted
As if they were parked in the middle
Of the street.

To Be My Girl

If I became terminally ill
I would make a call to an airline
And buy a round-trip ticket
To fly you out
And sit by my side
Just one day

When I graduate
I'll make a call to an airline
And buy a round-trip ticket
To fly you out
To watch me walk
And celebrate the day

If I fall asleep
I'll make a call to an airline
And buy a one-way ticket
To fly you out
To kiss my lips
To be my girl

When I wake up
I'll roll over to where you were
And find that you're not there
Too real a dream
To dream, so real
To be my girl

To Be Discontinued

love is trapped
love is restriction
love is tears of fire
love is a sickness
love is addiction and greed
love is kissing an empty bottle
love is running in place
love is staring into space
love is holographic
love is Valentine's Day
love is picturing
love is pressure
love is a red pill
love is desperation
love is 7 years of bad luck and broken glass
love is a watchpot
love is to be discontinued

Evan Mychal Smith

Traded In

I am to metal what steel is
what real is, cold
fearless? no

Dandelions pass off as roses
painting their noses red
weeds? never grow

Saturated in saccharine
taste, the apple has become grape
the real has become fake

I am to metal what copper feels
oxidized, ostracized
traded in for plastic

Vanilla Dreams

you give me vanilla dreams
motion pictures filled with scenes
of liplock, underneath sheets hips rock
to beats like hip-hop in sync like twin clocks
tick tock, one hand on six, the other nine
parallel spines, but inverted in design
not a crime for two friends, close
the most, amazing you are, no boast
a toast to us, to split you'd have to go through us
so tight a molecule couldn't flow through us
so air tight, so let me stare right, into your eyes
from close distance, wrapped around you
like quotes on a sentence
no period, cause there's no end to the story we
write
never ending, the glorious life

Evan Mychal Smith

Waiting In The Wind

I just stay still while you move me
Control me, release your fingertips
Throw me, and let me be
I'll catch a bus named destiny
Just let me see
What's left for me? or what's right?
Soul searching for light

I found me a bright source
I'll ride on in, come off of my horse
I'll pay what life costs
To give it chance, and plant seeds
And watch from stem grow leaves
Where we lay, sway and catch breeze

Speed I own not, nor direction
Only recognition of blown spot
Fighting air with waving arms to propel
Unable to prevail, heart swell
I must remain seated, grateful then
When I am carried in, I cascade and spin
Waiting in the wind

Walking with jeremy

nobody ever really dies
under the lemon yellow son
Jeremy the wicked twirls a wrist
intertwined with mine and together
we draw out our dreams

bones and blood for grass
inverted smiles and pain for joy
including all we knew and learned
whispers carried in the wind

birthday cake wishes unanswered
so this year, I'll blow pistols
smoking hot barrel of laughs
Jeremy finds it funny

we sit and talk, comparing eyes
stinging, red and swollen
he hands me a tissue
I refuse politely

a seizure in my pocket
my phone displays changing names
urgent, caring, prying
it's not for me

Evan Mychal Smith

Jeremy and I took a walk
talking along the way
I let it ring, not to be rude
having the time of my life

Warm company

it was written that the people will perish
for lack of knowledge, sinking in false bliss

to the depths with your thoughts
with your empty lives, devoid of fire

truth, like air, is our fuel to burn
to convert, to power, to rule

you are fools to let them lie
knowingly, violently, boastfully

they snicker behind your back
but you hear them too, don't you?

dancing to the music and reading the signs
tasting the venom and bearing the mark

connecting the circle
continuing the tradition

as the compass points eastward
you run toward the setting sun

toward the shackles and torment
docile, to die in warm company

We're good friends

I don't want to seem like a bad guy.
Because I'm not like the rest of them.
It may be hard not to believe me
Because of what I want you to do.
But it's really not that big of a deal.
I promise not to hurt you babe
And you know I wouldn't.
It's just that, I really need it.
I really need it babe.
I know we're good friends
And you don't want to ruin
The relationship we have
As caring, loving, friends.
But we don't have to be partners
To do what I want you to do
With me.
People do it all the time
Every day and night
With different people
And in different ways.
Just because we do this
Doesn't mean that it will change
How we will treat each other
Or how we feel about each other.
You will always be my friend
And I will always be yours.
So tell me what you think?
Even if we only do it once
I just really want you to

Let it happen between us.
Bring your body close
Until it can't get any closer
Look me in my eyes
Until we both understand
That the only thing
That can happen next
Is becoming one.
Mind, body
And soul.
Lean into me and let me have
What I've been waiting
So long for.
Your kiss.

Yell

Pre-cambrian bones in fossilized homes resides
above her self-respect
Which explains her clotting veins, the cookies on
the shelf, neglect
Her current state of fervent, late, now carry like a
servant plate
The curse of lips from serpent face, and taste from
her syrup and cake
I challenge you, oh public eye, to not judge me by
this reply
To wrongdoing I don't deny, but I shall not leave
these quotes aside
On second thought, I welcome rain, her name has
brought me naught but pain
She asked me what would it cost to change, forever
was her loss arranged
These tears of mine they leave me scars, they burn
for long, I need these bars
A prison cell in my own jail, incessant ringing, my
own bell

I'll hide these tears inside my skin, behind my eyes,
in my own sin
Like Daniel in the lion's den, residing where the
fire's been
Alluring as a maggot's squirm, but size that of a
pachyderm
Attractive as that "faggot" term, for her the lesson
has been learned

But now I know that running risk with honey from
a cunning witch
Is never worth the honey's drip, no joke is funny
from the lip
I've had my share of woe from this, still coping from
this choking grip
No rope and down the slope I slip, back up where
God I hope I fit

I may die before I'm understood, be locked away
under the wood
Instead of where the liars stood, be buried with the
highest good
This microscope with which I'm seen, is often
filthy, rarely clean
Of things I wouldn't dare to dream, I'm the accused,
nowhere to lean
A man stands tall, a man is strong, a man don't take
no mess for long
A man don't need no hand along, or someone to
understand his song
What man am I, who begs and pleads, who won't
give up on wants or needs
When under mask the hero bleeds and turns to ash
like Roman trees

Where senses lie where most have none
With peace signs where most have their guns
Where warmness lies where most are cold
Where open-hearted, most are closed

It seems my actions aren't speaking loud enough
So I'll yell to the sun through the clouds, I must!

Evan Mychal Smith

Echo my emotion and break every ear
Cause confusion and cause some fear
Hear me oh world, I'm done with your games
Falling in traps, being stuck on your trains
If only you knew what goes on in my head
You would let someone else suffer instead

Surely I can't be deserving this fate
The faster the clock spins, the earlier the date.

You, my savior

lurking in the shadow of Eden, the world
offers no protection, harnesses no guilt
and makes no promises. we wake into this
naked and confused, helpless and vulnerable

everything we are made of is born
after birth. every idiosyncrasy
all of our strengths, weaknesses
and all of our fears

into your arms I was delivered
the birthplace of a hero
surviving on your sacrifice
evidence of the grace of God
whom made you, my savior

i am constantly reborn
in your embrace and guided
by your wisdom so no matter
where i travel
you will always be home